BETSY ROSS

written and illustrated by

Alexandra Wallner

Holiday House / New York

Thanks to Theodore T. Newbold, Executive Director of American Flag House
and Betsy Ross Memorial, and Ann L. Tracey, researcher for the Betsy Ross
House, for their help.

Library of Congress Cataloging-in-Publication Data
Wallner, Alexandra.
Betsy Ross / written and illustrated by Alexandra Wallner.
—1st ed.
p.   cm.
Summary: An introduction to the life of the Philadelphia
seamstress credited with sewing the first American flag.
ISBN 0-8234-1071-4
1. Ross, Betsy, 1752–1836—Juvenile literature.
2. Revolutionaries—United States—Biography—Juvenile literature.
3. United States—History—Revolution, 1775–1783—Flags—Juvenile
literature. 4. Flags—United States—History—18th century—
Juvenile literature. [1. Ross, Betsy, 1752–1836.
2. Revolutionaries. 3. Flags—United States.] I. Title.
E302.6.R77W35   1994   93-3559   CIP   AC
973.3'092—dc20
[B]

For
John Dugdale,
the spirit
of my
colonial soul
~with love
A.W.

Elizabeth Griscom was born in Philadelphia, Pennsylvania on January 1, 1752. Elizabeth, called Betsy by her family, was the eighth child of seventeen born to Samuel and Rebecca. Her family were Quakers, a religious group that believed in living in a simple, peaceful way. The family was so large that the children had to help with chores. Betsy helped by sewing the white caps Quaker girls wore every day.

Betsy attended the Friends School with other Quakers and children from wealthy families. Besides learning reading, writing, arithmetic, geography, and history, students performed a four-hour task each day. Betsy used this time to sew. She enjoyed creating quilts and samplers with complicated designs. Betsy's needlework was the most beautiful in Philadelphia, and she won many prizes for it.

When Betsy was a teenager, she begged her parents to let her work outside their home. Her parents agreed to let her work for an upholsterer, sewing the coverings for sofas, chairs, and other furniture. In the shop, she met a worker named John Ross, and they fell in love. Betsy married him in 1773, even though he wasn't a Quaker. The Quakers and her parents disapproved of her marrying someone outside of the Quaker faith.

At this time, America was made up of only thirteen colonies on the East Coast, ruled by King George III of England. The Colonials did not like being under English rule. In 1775, their newly formed government, the Continental Congress, established an American army to fight the British. The first battles were fought in Lexington and Concord, Massachusetts, on April 19, 1775 and marked the beginning of the Revolutionary War.

Although Philadelphians knew about the fighting, business went on as usual. Betsy and John set up a small shop in 1775. They worked long hours to make their business succeed.

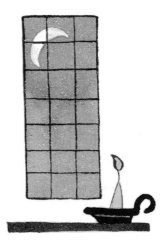

John joined the army. One night in 1776, he was guarding a storehouse full of ammunition that exploded. For months, Betsy nursed him with herbs and home remedies. Despite her care, John died.

Betsy was now a widow who ran her business alone in a shop on Arch Street. After work she made musket balls to help the American cause, going against the Quakers' peaceful ways.

General George Washington, the commander in chief of the army, wanted the Colonials to have a flag. Not only would it be a symbol of the Colonials' independence from England, it would also stand for the Colonies fighting together. He sketched a design for a flag and showed it to his close friends Robert Morris and Colonel George Ross. Colonel Ross, John's uncle, suggested that Betsy sew the flag.

The three men called on Betsy in her small shop.

When General Washington showed her his sketch, Betsy looked at it and frowned.

"Why not have a five-pointed star instead of a six-pointed one?" she said. "Five-pointed stars are easier to sew, and they waste less cloth."

The men looked doubtful, so she took a scrap of cloth, folded it, and with one snip of her scissors cut a five-pointed star.

"And I think the flag should be shaped like a rectangle. It would look better waving in the wind than the square flag drawn by General Washington."

The men were impressed by Betsy's design and agreed that it was better.

Betsy took great care in making the first American flag. She sewed thirteen stars shaped in a circle on a blue field. She placed it against thirteen red and white stripes.

On July 4, 1776, the Declaration of Independence was signed. The thirteen Colonies became the thirteen United States of America.

On June 14, 1777, Betsy's flag was described at a meeting of Congress and a resolution was passed. The minutes of the meeting read:

"Resolved, that the flag of the United States be thirteen stripes alternate red and white, that the union be thirteen stars in a blue field, representing a new constellation."

During the war, Betsy became well known for her beautiful flags, but her reputation as an upholsterer grew as well. She got many important jobs. She worked for Benjamin Franklin, the Society of Free Quakers, and the State House of Pennsylvania.

In 1777, Betsy married Joseph Ashburn, a sea captain. Joseph was often away from home. During one of his voyages, British soldiers occupied Philadelphia for a few months. Many citizens left the city, but Betsy stayed to run her business, even though she was alone. Soldiers camped in her house. She was polite to them, but she always let them know whose side she was on. The soldiers came to respect this lone, hardworking woman and called her "the Little Rebel."

During a sea battle with England, Joseph was taken prisoner. In 1782, when the war was over, Betsy learned from a friend named John Claypoole that Joseph had died in an English prison. Meanwhile, Betsy and Joseph's first child, Zillah, had died, and their second child, Elizabeth, had been born. Now Betsy was a widow again.

John Claypoole and Betsy's friendship grew. In 1783, John became Betsy's third husband.

They joined the Society of Free Quakers, which permitted marriage outside the faith. Betsy could worship in the church once again.

Together Betsy and John had five children: Clarissa, Susannah, Rachel, Jane, and Harriet, who died as a baby.

Although John was a sea voyager, Betsy asked him to come and work in her flourishing upholstery shop. She needed his help. But John grew bored with the upholstery business and went to work for the U.S. Customs House. He became ill the last few years of his life. John died in 1817.

Betsy taught sewing to her daughters, her granddaughters, and her nieces. When they grew up, they helped her run the business.

At age seventy-five, Betsy finally retired. Her eyesight was failing, and one of her children read the Bible to her as she sat by the fire. Betsy liked to tell stories about her life. Her favorite story was the one about making the first American flag.

Betsy died in 1836. The people who knew her told her story about the flag. Finally, in 1870, her grandson William J. Canby made Betsy's story public in an address to the Historical Society of Pennsylvania.

Betsy was buried on Arch Street in the garden of the house she once ran as an upholstery shop. The flag of the United States flies twenty-four hours a day over her grave.

AUTHOR'S NOTE

We know many facts about Betsy Ross's life, but there are also many conflicting stories. Some historians suggest that she won contests for her needlework. Others say she did not. Some historians do not agree that British soldiers were quartered in Betsy's home in 1777, although her grandniece Susan Satterthwaite Newport reported that not only were they there, they also referred to her as "the Little Rebel."

There is no absolute proof that Betsy Ross sewed the first American flag. The story of the flag commissioned by George Washington was passed down by Betsy's relatives and friends. However, George Washington, George Ross, and Robert Morris were in Philadelphia during the time that Betsy Ross said they came to her house. In 1963, Reeves Weatherill, a descendant of one of Betsy Ross's Colonial friends, Samuel Weatherill, presented a little paper star with the signature of Clarissa Claypoole Wilson at a luncheon of the Philadelphia Flag Day Association. Clarissa Claypoole carried on her mother's business after she died, and it is possible she gave Betsy Ross's famous star pattern to Samuel Weatherill.

In my version of Betsy Ross's story, I favored the accounts of her life in the book *The Truth About the Betsy Ross Story* by Robert Morris.

ALEXANDRA WALLNER

TO MAKE A STAR WITH FIVE POINTS

1

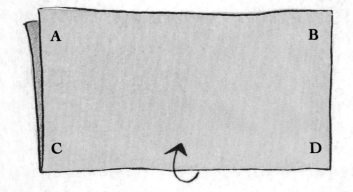

Fold a square of paper in half, like this.

3

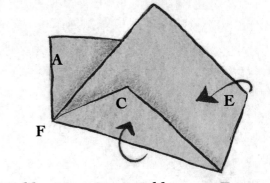

Fold corner C up. Fold corner E over to F.

2

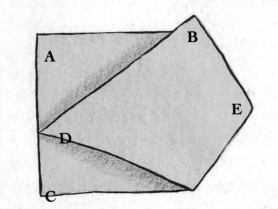

Fold corner D to a halfway point between A + C.

4

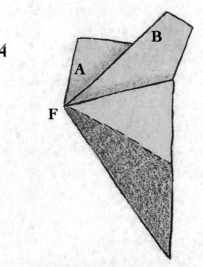

Cut through all layers along dotted line. Unfold shaded area to make star.